Sales Value Propositions

Sales Value Propositions

The Cutting Edge

Terry Barge

Business-to-Business Sales Strategist
for High-Performing Sales Teams

DAGMAR
MIURA
LOS ANGELES

Sales Value Propositions: The Cutting Edge

For more information, you can contact the author at either terrybarge1@gmail.com or via his profile page on LinkedIn.

Dagmar Miura
Los Angeles
www.dagmarmiura.com

First published 2018

ISBN: 978-1-942267-82-9

This book is dedicated to my lovely wife, Ellie, who has been my constant encourager, supporter, and advisor throughout the complete process of producing this book

"Victory can be crafted."
—Sun Tzu, *The Art of War*

Contents

Foreword
The Client's View

The Sales Value Proposition (SVP) is the most important part of identifying what makes your company and the solutions you sell different from your competitors.

In my experience, without an understanding of how to write successful SVPs, salespeople are drawn into the technology and price argument, as this is then the only differentiator. The consequence of this process results in a price war, devaluing the solution and not meeting the customers' needs.

Since my sales team have learned the technique of writing a successful SVP, they now have the tools to clearly differentiate themselves by understanding the customer and their requirements, whilst demonstrating credibility and a return on investment.

The SVP process has changed the way my team communicates with prospects and customers.

Mark Berry
Sales Director, Jade Solutions (UK) Limited
www.jade-solutions.co.uk

Introduction
A Most Powerful
Sales Tool

———◆———

"A company's value proposition … must be
intuitive, so that a customer can read or hear the
value proposition and understand the delivered
value without further explanation."
— www.investopedia.com

Sales Value Propositions (SVPs) are among the most powerful sales tools available to business-to-business salespeople, when it comes to initiating and sustaining credibility and rapport with customers.

At the same time, SVPs are among the most frequently overlooked and underutilised tools by sales and marketing professionals at every level of an organisation.

The impact on organisational and individual sales effectiveness and ultimate performance is, in my view, significant.

My observations are not designed to be a criticism of

professional selling as a whole. They are made specifically with respect to the application of SVPs and the pivotal role they play as vitally important business communication tools appropriate at every level and at every stage of every sales and marketing initiative.

Yes, SVPs are that important.

In the current sales environment – which is, from a customer standpoint, extremely demanding, and from a competitive perspective, extremely hostile – sales executives and their teams need, as a matter of some urgency, to bring into play all the potential advantages that SVPs provide. Currently, however, that's simply not happening to any great extent.

In my experience, there are a number of reasons for this:

- An incomplete knowledge of the real function of Sales Value Propositions
- Misunderstanding about the versatility of SVPs, from their higher-level strategic application to the more routine, opportunity-based tactical application
- Inability to create an SVP so that the impact on key individuals or larger and more disparate audiences is credible, persuasive, and motivating
- The absence of real discipline and skill, to consult and uncover the key information that is vital to the quality and ultimate effectiveness of an SVP
- A "silo" mentality that severely limits the effectiveness of SVPs by placing its oversight in a specific department like Marketing or Sales, where "never the twain shall meet"

In the following chapters we'll explore and overcome many of the issues that obscure the importance of SVPs and prevent them from playing a far more prominent role in building credibility, trust, and competitive advantage for yourselves and your companies. Credibility is the vital ingredient when building trust with a customer.

A key function of SVPs is enabling credibility to be established quickly, effectively, and with integrity in the minds of your customers, in their decision-making, and in their subsequent actions.

"Take a minute and think about one person who could really help boost your business. Now, what would you say to them? You only have a few seconds of their attention. How would you get the light bulb to go off in their mind? How would you convince them that you are worth working with, investing in, or talking about? In this moment, the difference between an 'A-ha!' and an 'Oh … interesting' is huge."
—Andrea Goulet Ford, CEO, Corgibytes

CHAPTER ONE

What Is a Sales Value Proposition?

———•———

> "People won't ever buy from you if they don't even understand why they should pay attention to you. And they notice you only if you have a strong value proposition."
> —Peter Sandeen, Kissmetrics

The phrase "value proposition" is credited to Michael Lanning and Edward Michaels, who first used the term in a 1988 staff paper for the consulting firm McKinsey and Co, entitled "A business is a value delivery system …"

I've taken the liberty of preceding the phrase with the word "sales," because my main objective is emphasising its role as a customer-centric tool, the primary aim of which is to create and drive momentum at every stage of the sales process.

Let's get started with a definition of an SVP that will help get our voyage of discovery underway:

A Sales Value Proposition is a concise, tailored statement which describes the customer's business pain, its operational impact, and its economic cost. It explains the measurable results the customer gets from implementing your solution and how your solution stands out from other offerings, using anecdotal evidence to prove its effectiveness.

Note: The word "pain" is used from time to time throughout this book. It's frequently used in sales to describe an issue, a challenge, a problem, a crisis, or a difficulty.

So let's break that definition down into some key characteristics that describe an SVP:

- It's a statement which can be communicated verbally and in writing.
- It's concise, so it gets to the point quickly.
- It's tailored and not generic.
- It's versatile, so customers and prospects both qualify as legitimate targets.
- It describes a business pain, its operational impact, and economic cost.
- It explains the solution and how it resolves the business pain, its operational impact, and its economic cost.
- It shows how the solution stands out from other offerings by either highlighting its uniqueness or how it's significantly different from other offerings.
- It defines a measurable Return on Investment for the customer.
- It reassures the customer that you have resolved similar business issues effectively in the past.

Occasionally, salespeople ask me if SVPs aren't really about "something we are doing all the time anyway."

Understanding the customer's business situation, developing a solution, trying to differentiate from competitors, and using testimonials do form a regular part of the day-to-day life of every professional salesperson.

There are no great surprises here; the world of SVPs draws on very familiar sales issues, the usual competitive challenges, and well-known marketing concepts.

So, you're asking, what's new then?

What's new has evolved from the unprecedented sales challenges still reverberating in the marketplace from the aftershocks of the global recession of 2008.

"Selling today in the corporate sector takes place in an environment that is volatile, uncertain, complex, and ambiguous. As never before, the sales professional must react and adapt to the nature and change in business."
—"Buyers' View of Salespeople," TACK International

This changed marketplace presents every salesperson with unique and contemporary challenges, especially when it comes to communicating business value to customers and prospects in a way that resonates with them, quickly and persuasively.

What's also new is that SVPs are playing an increasingly central role in successfully tackling these tough communication challenges.

From a sales viewpoint, though, it takes a very different kind of mindset and a significant improvement in skill to create and apply SVPs effectively.

Initially the challenge is about the salesperson's insight and ingenuity as they home in on the most critical sales information swirling about on their business intelligence radar.

The successful salesperson is always able to answer the question:

> "What sales information is the most important when it comes to creating a compelling SVP?"

The significant improvement in skill comes in crafting

that critical sales information into a value-based positioning statement that quickly connects and appeals to both customers and prospects.

So, the world of SVPs is about taking what appears to be familiar and skilfully and creatively transforming it into a powerful, value-based message that gets a really positive response from either the reader or the listener:

"I get the message; we have to talk!"

"People will buy from you if you are able to cut to the chase. Tell them what they will get. ... Don't bore them. Be precise."
— Robert Craven, MD, The Directors' Centre

An Account Manager attended my one-day "Communicating Unique Business Value" workshop. As part of the learning process, teams of salespeople develop SVPs for real-time, "live" sales opportunities they have brought to the workshop.

In the pre-workshop briefing, the participants are encouraged to bring sales opportunities that are either stalled, or are so competitive that there's a real need to re-examine the sales plan, create additional business value, and improve competitive advantage.

The Account Manager's situation was that he had a solid business solution to a particular customer's business issue and no obvious competition. His challenge was that every time he met with the business principal, their meeting was constantly interrupted. He explained that the customer was in a furniture manufacturing business, where the business principal was very hands-on.

The Account Manager had done everything he could to make their regular meetings successful – setting the appointment well ahead of time, creating an agenda, making pre-meeting phone calls, and confirming the key points for discussion. Their meetings, though, were constantly punctuated by phone calls, customers needing attention in the factory store, and production issues on the manufacturing side. The Account Manager had become quite frustrated with what were clearly well-intentioned but ultimately dysfunctional meetings.

In an attempt to deal with the challenge, the group helped him develop a very polished SVP and some creative ideas about how he could use it with the customer.

A short time later, I ran a review session with the group to get feedback on how they had been using the SVPs that had been created in the workshop.

Our Account Manager was among the first to contribute his feedback. He proceeded to relate a fascinating story of how he had used the SVP and the outcome it had achieved.

He had used his usual approach to set up the meeting. They agreed on the date and time of the meeting, put it in both their calendars, and he shared a meeting agenda – however, this time with one key difference. He inserted the SVP created in the workshop at the top of the meeting agenda as a kind of "mission statement" for the meeting.

When he called the customer later to confirm the meeting, he was very pleasantly surprised. The customer told him that their meeting would be at the warehouse because, as the business principal put it, "we'll get some peace and quiet there." Needless to say, the result was a very productive meeting.

The Account Manager was convinced that the SVP's precise, tailored messaging had made a decisive contribution in capturing the customer's attention. That messaging led to a far more effective meeting and ultimately helped to deliver a successful sales outcome.

"The power of language to influence how people behave should never be underestimated."
—Mick Cope, *The Seven Cs of Consulting*

CHAPTER TWO

Why Do You Need a Sales Value Proposition?

———◆———

> "Your business's value proposition is arguably the most important element of your overall marketing messaging. A value proposition tells prospects why they should do business with you rather than your competitors, and makes the benefits of your products or services crystal clear from the outset."
> —WordStream: Online Advertising Made Easy

Organisations invest a lot of resources creating corporate statements designed to define, among other things, their brand, clarify their mission, communicate their values and beliefs, and describe their vision.

These are usually relatively short, concise statements that tell anyone who cares to listen what kind of business the organisation is, where it is headed, its range of products and services, its target marketplace, and if you're lucky, what

13

makes it unique and the preferred choice of its customers.

When these statements are all connected you probably have a reasonably clear idea of the organisation's identity and its credentials; a little like a corporate résumé.

Upon closer examination, it doesn't take long to work out the common focus of all these corporate statements: they all tend to be, for the most part, *inward*-looking.

So, if you're like me and start to look around for a well-rounded SVP, you'll be very fortunate if you find one. If you then inquire of somebody who looks like they might know about the whereabouts of the company SVP, you're likely to receive a reply that goes something like,

"Oh, you mean our elevator pitch?"

"Not really!" is my usual reply.

There are some similarities between an SVP and an Elevator Pitch. They are both concise statements, designed to be memorable and to create some degree of initial rapport and credibility between the presenter and the listener. However, they are fundamentally different in terms of content and focus.

The Elevator Pitch is a short, snappy statement that leads mainly with the presenter's organisational credentials and is **inward-looking.**

The SVP is a short, snappy statement that leads mainly with the customer's business priorities and is **outward-looking.**

So, back in the elevator, you've established your business credentials with an important individual – a decision-maker or an "influencer." Using your elevator pitch, you've sent a clear message to that individual that you're worth listening to.

So what's next?

Remember you're still in the elevator so you need to get to the point quickly and your message has to make a positive impact. You want to make an impressive connection with your customer or prospect and earn the right to a bigger chunk of quality time, during which you can consult more, learn more, and convey an even more compelling story.

Decision time has arrived. Do you continue with an inward-looking, product-based narrative – or do you have something at your fingertips that's much more customer-centric? Do you have a value-based hook that will grab and keep the customer's attention?

If you have a tailored and relevant SVP ready and waiting, you're in great shape. As we've already seen, a key characteristic of an SVP is its powerful combination of conciseness and precision.

If you don't, then you are probably about to wander off down "Product and Price Boulevard," which will likely turn out to be a dead-end street.

So why is there this pressing need to get to the point quickly?

Well, you've probably worked hard to get in front of an important individual at a valued customer or target prospect; however you also know that getting the appointment is only half of the battle.

You are still going to be confronted by more challenges:

• People's lives are very busy and fast-moving, especially senior executives'.
• Business and personal priorities are constantly changing.
• Your competitors are trying to gain access at your expense.
• Your message is just one of many trying to be heard.
• The impact you need is so easily diminished in this daily cacophony of competing voices and messages.

"Buyers have evolved. Overwhelmed with an increasing number of choices, buyers are no longer willing to wait patiently for sales reps to make that perfect pitch."
Qvidian's "2015 State of Sales Execution Report"

It's a time and attention issue with which you are competing – you have to be ready with a concise, customer-centric message delivered with optimal impact.

One of the easier places to illustrate where you see the attention-grabbing power of conciseness and precision is at the movies.

Picture the scene: you've settled down in the theatre in your nice, comfortable seat, and are waiting to be entertained. But before the feature film plays, you're going to suffer a barrage of mildly entertaining commercials – and then, as your impatience starts to rise, you're presented with a series of trailers of movies to be shown at the theatre in the near future. Fortunately, they are usually a little more entertaining than the commercials!

So what's this interruption all about? What's the aim of a trailer?

Well, very simply, to persuade you and the rest of the captive audience in the theatre to give up some more of your leisure time and money to watch the movie – in their theatre, they hope.

So what do they show you in the trailer? Some of best bits! So there you have it, in a nutshell.

An SVP is a really well-constructed "trailer" that describes some of the best bits of your business proposal, and is designed specifically to motivate your listeners and readers to want to see your full movie!

"Complexity is your enemy. Any fool can make something complicated. It is hard to make something simple."
—Richard Branson

In 2006, I was working with a major British bank that wanted to bring an upgraded level of professional selling to its national team of business services consultants.

We had already covered in previous workshops most of

the core sales skills and activities that the team needed for the upgrade. Among those skills was the role and development of SVPs.

A little while later, we regrouped to review the progress that each consultant had made in implementing some of the new sales approaches. There were, as always in these kinds of sessions, some great stories and anecdotes of commercial success and personal growth. However, one story in particular made a real impression on the whole group.

The consultant told us of how he had been given the responsibility of introducing two new bank products to potential business prospects in his territory. He emphasized that these prospects were genuine new business targets and not current clients of the bank.

He went on to say that his first objective was to get an appointment with each prospect, for a meeting in which he could spend quality time doing some face-to-face selling. His normal approach, he said, would have been very "product-focused," when making that initial telephone call.

He would make the call, equipped with all of the product's features, and then try to convince the prospect that this product was something about which they should really learn more. Then, at an opportune moment, he would try to make the appointment.

Following our training sessions, he had decided to try a different approach. As part of his pre-call planning, he fashioned tailored SVPs based on the business issues the two financial products were designed to resolve, and the corresponding benefits and business value each could deliver.

He crafted some consultative questions to lead off his telephone call. His simple objective was to discover if his prospect was actually experiencing the issues for which he already knew his products were the potential solution. Once his prospect confirmed they had the business need, he then delivered his pre-designed SVP to secure a face-to-face meeting.

He concluded his story by telling us how many of his initial telephone calls he had converted into face-to-face meetings – his strike rate was, at that time, 100 percent.

"The business revolution is sweeping away many of the traditional ways of working, of interacting with customers. If we don't change, if we don't embrace the future, we will be left behind."
—Larry Wilson, *Stop Selling, Start Partnering*

CHAPTER THREE

Creating Sales Value Propositions

———◆———

> "Information means getting facts – timely, accurate facts about the reality of conditions and circumstances in the competitive situation. Nothing in competition is more important than obtaining facts."
> —Donald Krause, *The Art of War for Executives*

Effective selling is a function of how much you really know about what's going on in the key areas of your sales environment – information providing power.

Effective SVPs take that information an important stage further. They are a function of how much *specific* insight you have about your customer's business situation, your competitors, and your own distinctive capabilities – critical and deeper insight providing you with formidable leverage.

In my book, *Selling Strategically: A 21st-Century Playbook,* I introduced the role of the Sales Strategist. This is the role that epitomizes what it takes to be a successful business-to-business salesperson meeting the challenges of the

19

current business environment.

So that there's no doubt about the vital nature of the information-gathering and consulting skills needed to build effective SVPs, I will summarise the four specific skill areas of the Sales Strategist.

The Business Consultant

The Business Consultant's role is to gain accurate insights into the customer or prospect's business and marketplace situation.

The aim is to have a clear understanding of the customer and prospect's strategic goals and objectives, and to know in what way they define the organisational vision of business success.

Sales attention can then focus on those pains that are barriers to the achievement of business success, especially those that represent current and future sales opportunities.

> Objective: "Where's the pain, what's its impact, what's its cost?"

The Relationship Manager

The Relationship Manager's role is to identify those internal or external individuals who control or significantly influence the customer's decision-making process, and to orchestrate effective relationships with them.

These individuals also contribute to and validate the insights the Business Consultant has acquired about each customer or prospect's business situation.

> Objective: "Who are the primary targets for my SVP?"

The Competitor Analyst

The Competitor Analyst's role is pivotal, as successful selling relies on accurate competitive intelligence.

In order to be successful, the Sales Strategist will need to outthink and outmanoeuvre competitors and create competitive advantage through genuine differentiation.

The Competitor Analyst's role is focused on assessing each competitor's strengths and weaknesses, from the information provided by the Business Consultant and Relationship Manager

> Objective: "What will it take for us to be seen as different from our competitors?"

The Solutions Provider

The Solutions Provider creates effective solutions based on the strategic intelligence gathered by the Business Consultant, the Relationship Manager, and the Competitor Analyst.

Selecting the relevant capabilities and resources, the Solutions Provider embeds them in a differentiated solution that will resolve the pains that are seen as barriers to the customer's business success.

> Objective: "What will it take to fix the pain, its impact and cost in a distinctive way?

"A balanced value proposition is the basis for brand choice and customer loyalty, and is critical to the ongoing success of a firm."
—Chris Allen, Thomas O'Guinn, and Richard Semenik, *Advertising and Integrated Brand Promotion*

The Five Stages of the SVP

These are the five stages that make up the structure of an SVP. We'll work with each of them in turn:

1. The Customer's Pain, Its Impact and Its Cost

2. The Solution
3. Differentiation
4. The Customer's Return on Investment
5. Anecdotal Evidence

This fixed structure is designed to embody the "best bits" of your "trailer" and fit within the time frame of thirty to forty-five seconds and enables us to meet two critical SVP criteria: precision and conciseness.

The five stages also enable us to respond three fundamental questions that every customer and prospect is asking – whether they realise it or not!

1. Why should I buy your product or service?
   Do you really know what I need and why?

2. What's so different about you?
   Why should I prefer you to any other supplier?

3. What's in it for me?
   What is the financial payoff?

In the following chapters we'll examine the key thought processes for each of the five stages enabling you, piece-by-piece, to create tailored SVPs for every sales situation you are likely to encounter.

CHAPTER FOUR

Stage One – The Customer's Pain, Impact and Cost

At whatever point in the sales process we pitch our SVP; this stage will always need to be the primary focus of our attention. Everything flows from this pivotal point.

- What's the customer's business pain?
- What are the effects on the business operationally?
- What's the current and ongoing economic cost?

This stage also constitutes the largest proportion of the SVP. We're aiming for around forty to forty five per cent of the total time to be devoted to Stage One.

This would mean between fifteen and twenty seconds, depending on the length of the overall SVP itself. Remember, an SVP deals with one customer pain and one solution at a time. If you really want to confuse the customer and everybody else, try creating SVPs that contain more than one core pain!

I've been asked by salespeople why we kick off the SVP

telling the customer something that they must already know – their business problem, its effect, and its cost. It's a great question.

One good reason is that the customer hasn't always thought the problem all the way through the pain, impact, and cost process for themselves.

Often, it's going to be the responsibility of a salesperson to help facilitate the process with the customer and highlight the importance of fixing the problem and the negative consequences of doing nothing.

In my experience, few salespeople can clearly articulate a pain, impact, and cost statement, which goes a long way to clarifying the customer's business situation. The salesperson that does will always create significant credibility with their customer.

The major reason we kick off the SVP with a pain, impact, and cost statement is not that the customer doesn't necessarily know, but *they need to know that YOU KNOW!*

It's a pivotal credibility-building statement that tells the customer you care about their agenda, their priorities, and what success means to them, and that you are fully aware of those legendary "keeps them awake at night" issues.

"One thing we've discovered with certainty is that anything we do that makes the customer more successful inevitably results in a financial return for us."
—Jack Welch with Suzy Welch, *Winning*

So what does a pain, impact, and cost statement look like?

Here's an example. Remember, simplicity is the key; do not overcomplicate it.

"We agreed earlier that your retention rates have fallen for the past three years from 90 percent to the current level of 80 percent, due to a complete lack of contact with customers over the period of their annual contract.

"This means that over that same period your business has lost about 500 customers.

"With an average customer spend of £450 each year; around £200,000 of revenue has been lost."

1. What's the core pain?
   A complete lack of contact with customers over the period of their annual contract.

2. What are the effects?
   Retention rates have fallen for the past three years from 90 percent to the current level of 80 percent. The business has lost about 500 customers.

3. What's the cost?
   Around £200,000 of revenue has been lost.

This statement looks simple enough when it's written down, however we need to reflect on the consulting, the questioning, and the research that's taken place to get to an understanding of what's really going on with this customer's business situation.

The consulting process is essential in order to describe this particular customer's situation in a simple, concise, but nonetheless accurate fashion.

"People often associate complexity with deeper meaning, when often after precious time has been lost, it is realized that simplicity is the key to everything."
—Gary Hopkins, www.findingsource.com

Now you're going to try this for yourself!

Focus on a current sales opportunity where you need to create more competitive advantage so you can make progress. It may be that your opportunity has lost momentum because the customer's attention is elsewhere, and you need to breathe some life into it before it expires completely.

The Business Pain

What's the core customer pain? What issue needs to be fixed?

Be careful here, because you are most likely to start with an "effect" of something or a symptom and not the real core pain.

In our example, the retention rate and the loss of customers were both painful, but they were symptoms of a deeper problem. The core pain turned out to be the complete lack of any contact with customers during the contract period.

So when you have identified some pain, keep asking yourself the question "What's causing that pain?" until you reach the legitimate cause.

The Customer pain for my sales opportunity is:

_____

_____

_____

The Business Impact of the Pain

The good news is that having gone through the cause and effect process, you have probably identified some of the operational impacts already. It's not unusual to have more than one impact from the single customer pain.

A point to make here is that gaining a clear insight of the true impact of a business pain will usually mean talking to more than one person in the customer's organisation. Depending on the type of pain, other departments and individuals will be affected.

Some of these individuals will also have a role in the decision-making process, either as a decision-maker or key influencer, which means their feedback and opinions carry weight – don't overlook them! Their perspective about the impact and cost are essential to creating a credible and persuasive SVP.

So a key question to ask from the outset should be "Who else should I be talking to about this pain?" "Who else is it affecting?"

In our original example we identified two primary impacts:

1. Falling retention rates
2. Loss of customers

I regularly see three or four legitimate impacts of a single pain in the many hundreds of sales situations that have been brought to the workshops.

Here is an example of one core pain where you will see at least seven operational impacts.

My client was selling materials to a road surfacing company, who in turn was contracted to a UK public-sector authority. The contractor had been using a competitor's product, which was cheaper and less reliable than the one supplied by my client. Although the cheaper material had proved to be very unsatisfactory, my client was still under pressure from the contractor to reduce the price of its higher-quality product.

In the workshop, the sales team saw a clear opportunity to begin moving the narrative away from price by working through the pain, impact and cost process. They saw how important it was to get a clear sense of the true cost to the contractor of using poor materials, and from that position demonstrate the true value of their superior product.

The example that follows contains the actual sales opportunity data that was brought to the workshop and demonstrates excellent research and consulting work by the Account Manager.

Here's how that first element of their SVP played out:

"Your current utility reinstatements have a high level of failure, typically 60+ percent, caused by poor compaction. These failures result in rework costs, local authority fines, loss of productivity, and loss of reputation with the client, together with disruption to the public."

The core pain here is the poor compaction of the inferior materials.

The actual and potential impacts, though, are very significant:

1. A high level of failure
2. Utility reinstatements
3. Rework costs
4. Local authority penalties
5. Loss of productivity
6. Loss of reputation
7. Disruption to the public

Already you can see the benefits of opening up the impact of the core problem and uncovering a number of important underlying impact issues.

Let's go back to your opportunity and assess the impacts:

The business impacts of my customer's pain are:

1. _____

2. _____

3. _____

The Cost of the Pain

In our original example of the pain, impact, and cost statement, we were able to identify an overriding cost to the customer of the business pain *because* we identified the impacts. We knew that retention rates were falling and we were able to calculate how many customers overall had been lost and the average value of their contracts.

Five hundred customers had failed to renew their contracts over the three-year period. The typical contract value was £450, which meant that over £200,000 of revenue had been lost.

Of course, some of you would have already spotted the fact that £200,000 of revenue is only what has been lost so far.

For a customer who might be still uncertain about fixing the problem, you could legitimately extrapolate the trend into the future and demonstrate the additional financial consequences of doing nothing – a very persuasive approach!

Clarifying these impacts is hugely important, not only because they are the most significant credibility-builders of the whole SVP, but because they start the all-important value-based narrative that immediately reduces the focus on price.

Let's return to the earlier real-time example, where the sales situation becomes a lot clearer by looking at the cost implications of this large number of impacts:

1. High level of failure
   The 60 percent failure rate told the Account Manager how many failures had occurred.

2. Utility reinstatements and rework costs
   The Account Manager knew the average rework cost for each failure was between £300 and £800 per repair.

3. Local authority penalties
   Penalties here refer to issues like overruns on the timetable for completion of the repairs, any further repair failures, and disruptions to the community. These kinds of penalties sometimes run into millions of pounds.

4. Loss of productivity
   The genuine loss of productivity here relates to the new revenue-generating projects the contractors' personnel could be working on if they were not tied up with the rework. This is not so easy to quantify at first sight, however it is possible by quantifying the hourly rate of the personnel and the lost revenue from the new projects.

5. Loss of reputation

If the contractor's failure reflects badly on the ultimate local authority customer and demeans its reputation, then the customer will likely show the contractor the exit door, along with all the future revenue and profit – potentially a huge cost.

The pain, impact, cost exercise breathed new life into the price-pressured sales opportunity and more confidence into the Account Manager. The higher cost of his product became a virtual non-issue when compared to the actual and potential costs of using the competitor's inferior materials.

It also demonstrated to everyone in the room why this opening statement is so pivotal to the SVP's effectiveness and impact.

Let's go back to your original sales opportunity and assess the various costs associated with the impacts of the core pain on your customer.

The costs of the business impacts are:

1. _____

2. _____

3. _____

So now you can put the three exercises together – the pain, the impact, and the costs.

Combine them to make your SVP's opening statement. It might sound a little clunky at first, but work on it until it flows.

Now check your timing – it should take around fifteen to twenty seconds to present at a normal speaking pace. The timing is important because the customer needs to get a clear message from the outset that you have their business priorities centre stage – that's the hook.

If it takes longer, wordsmith it back until it fits the time

frame. If it's shorter, you may not have developed the opening SVP statement enough; usually it's the impact section
that needs to be developed further.

CHAPTER FIVE

Stage Two –
The Solution

If ever the word "discipline" meant anything, it's here at Stage Two. Conciseness is all and everything at this particular stage.

If your SVP is going to miss the mark, it's probably here where you will be desperate to drone on and on and on … and on about your products and services.

Even if you have done a great job at Stage One, you will blow it right here if you don't restrain yourself. As with every great trailer, you don't want to give the whole plot away.

So don't spend a disproportionate amount of SVP time describing endless product features and technical complexities. It's not necessary – remember, it's the trailer!

So why does this fixation with our products exist at all?

The main reason is that that we are far more familiar with our own products and services than with the customer or prospect's business priorities.

In workshops I often see pain, impact, and cost statements at Stage One that are very sketchy, whilst the solution statements here at Stage Two are a veritable *War and Peace.*

One of the reasons I drive salespeople crazy in workshops

is by rigorously enforcing the Stage One and Two timings. Frequently, it's the only way to get the balance right!

However, we need to be thorough in developing our solution statement. We need to describe, albeit briefly, how it will resolve the pain and its impact.

An effective first step in building a business solution is focusing on more than just the core products and services that you sell.

I cover this more expansive way of thinking in more detail in *Selling Strategically*, but I'll summarise here because it's relevant.

At Stage One we saw that salespeople can have a limited view of the customer's business situation, maybe knowing the pain but not pushing on in the consulting process to the impact and cost. This restricted vision also affects how business solutions are constructed; often the brainstorming process doesn't go much further than the products and services on the price list.

Here is a four-step approach to expanding our vision of the wider range of organisational capabilities that will add a lot more business value to your solution.

The 4 Ps

Products are the obvious place to start and where you are most knowledgeable. What products and services do you actually sell? What's on your price list? Which specific product features, benefits, and advantages will add real value to the solution for the opportunity you have selected?

Next we need to look at **People** – as great sources of potential value. Companies like PWC and KPMG are built almost entirely around their people, their experience, their specialist skills, and their expertise. Where are the talented, experienced people in your organisation who will add real value to your solution?

Let's move onto customer-facing **Processes**. The current marketplace is filled with companies who focus on processes as the major component of value. Amazon, Uber, and Airbnb have created significant market impact focusing on process, not just products. Which organisational processes will add real value to your solution?

The fourth solution source is **Partners**. Building effective solutions will mean looking outside your own organisation for incremental business value and competitive advantage.

Technology companies promote Intel, eBay promotes PayPal, high street stores offer credit card payments, airlines promote car hire companies, and washing machine companies promote detergents.

Each of these represents well-known partnerships and they will provide extra value for their customers. Which partners will add incremental value to your solution?

Let's take a look at our example again, but this time with the solution piece completed.

"We agreed earlier that your retention rates have fallen for the past three years from 90 percent to the current level of 80 percent, due to a complete lack of contact with customers over the period of their annual contract.

"This means that over that same period your business has lost about 500 customers. With an average customer spend of £450 each year; around £200,000 of revenue has been lost.

> "Combining our proprietary digital technology with our experienced sales team, each customer will be contacted quarterly about special offers and the financial benefits of contract renewal."

That's about all you need – around seven to ten seconds' worth of time. Beyond ten seconds and you're going too far.

You want the customer or prospect to react by wanting to invest more time with you, to engage more and learn more; it's then that you can expand on your solution's features and benefits.

To engage with decision-makers and influencers, you have to earn the right to a bigger chunk of their valuable time. That is the primary role of the SVP; it's the vehicle for achieving just that.

Remember earlier we said we're looking for this kind of initial response:

"I really get the message; we have to talk!"

In our example we have included a **Product**, the technology software. It's digital, so there is in all probability **Process** embedded in the software, and the **People** are represented by the experienced sales team.

Now it's your turn. Review your pain, impact, and cost statement for your opportunity. Consider the 4 Ps.

Describe what your proposed solution is:

My solution is:

_____

_____

_____

How long did it take to read aloud your solution section? If it's over ten seconds then get brutal and reduce it down to no more than eight seconds.

So now you have completed the first two SVP stages, and you should have created a clear connection between the two by describing concisely and accurately how your solution fixes the customer's pain, impact, and cost.

You've now created a really good definition of "business value" by answering one of the three questions we looked at earlier:

Why should I buy your product or service?

CHAPTER SIX

Stage Three – Differentiation

—————◆—————

> "Your prospects have one basic question: What makes you so different that I should do business with you? Your prospects are making the classic statement: Give me one good reason why."
> —Harry Beckwith, Selling the Invisible

Now we need to push on and look for "unique business value," or at least "differentiated business value."

We have to break away from the "Me Too" brigade. Our solution has to stand out from the crowd and provide a convincing response to the questions:

What's so different about you? Why should I prefer you to any other supplier?

You may not realise it, but you've already covered some key areas of potential differentiation already.

Differentiation because you are aligned with your customer's business priorities

Developing the pain, impact, and cost statement will, all by itself distinguish you from the majority of your competitors.

Many of your rivals will simply be too lazy, will not have spent the time or done the research necessary to fully understand the customer's business situation.

Don't underestimate the respect that customers will give you for doing your "homework" and aligning with their business priorities.

Remember what we said at Stage One: The major reason we kick off the SVP with a pain, impact, and cost statement is not that the customer doesn't necessarily know, but that *they need to know that YOU KNOW!*

I was discussing the issue of understanding the customer's business priorities with a group of account managers in financial services, when I was interrupted by the Sales Director.

He said, "Let me give you an example, to clarify the importance of aligning with the client's priorities first and not focusing on your own sales priorities."

He named a client, a very big insurance brokerage that represented about £10 million of sales for my client each year. They shared the relationship with the brokerage with a major competitor. Despite their best efforts, they had not been able to find a way to become sole supplier. They had an excellent relationship with the client, but every time they attempted to win all of the business, the Managing Partner simply said, "I need to keep you both on your toes, that's why you both have a share of my business."

However, without warning, they received a Request for Proposal from the client, asking them to submit a proposal to handle all of the brokerage's business. They completed their proposal and sent it to the client. About a week later, they got the response telling them that they had not been successful.

Shocked, they telephoned the client to try to retrieve the situation but were told the decision was final. They asked if they could discuss why they had lost the bid, a request that was granted.

The Sales Director and the Account Manager visited the

client to find out exactly why they had lost the business. They were told that it was a tough decision, but a key element of their offering seemed not to cover a particular procedure that was important to the client's cashflow.

The competitor had specifically highlighted this process in their proposal, putting it among one of the key features of their solution. It was this element that had swayed their thinking and determined the final decision.

I could tell the room was restless. The Sales Director noticed and he said, "I know what you're thinking!" He told the room, "We thought the same thing – we did do that, and it's in our proposal!"

He made that same point to the client, showing them that very feature in their proposal. It was on a page quite near the end of the document.

The client's response was quite blunt: "We didn't get that far!"

The difference between the two proposals was quite clear: knowing the client's priorities was one thing, demonstrating it so the client knew that they knew was quite another.

The winning bid was not based on a superior product; it was based on demonstrating a superior insight of the customer's priorities.

Differentiation because your company's full range of value-adding capabilities are in play

"The world has a surplus of similar companies, employing similar people, with similar educational backgrounds working in similar jobs, coming up with similar ideas, producing similar things, with similar prices and similar quality."
—Tom Peters, Business Guru, *The World Economic Forum*

The 4 Ps exercise is a simple but nonetheless illuminating exercise that I facilitate in every workshop.

I say "illuminating" because the exercise frequently produces some very interesting reactions from salespeople in the room.

- "I had no idea we could do that … "
- "What is that exactly?"
- "I've never heard of that particular service … "
- "The Finance Director came on the call with you?"
- "We deliver on weekends?"
- "We can actually finance that?"

Most salespeople have a reasonable grasp of their company's core products and services, or at least the ones they are responsible for selling. Beyond that, other organisational capabilities – especially customer-facing processes and the skills and experience of our talented people – are frequently regarded as, "Well, it's what we do, isn't it?"

We need to stop discarding these additional sources of value because they are a literal treasure trove of potential differentiation. We have to become smarter and make better use of the full range of our organisation's capabilities.

The 4 Ps exercise brings into play far more of an organisation's value-based capabilities than most salespeople normally consider. By "playing with a full deck" you can, in my experience, create a genuine perception in the mind of the customer that you are legitimately different.

Your competitors might be able to do the same, but if they can't be bothered to highlight the fact then you are going to be seen as different by default! This is precisely what happened in our previous story and the consequences were disastrous.

The Sales Director of a major global technology company asked me to support its two-day launch of a Managed Services offering. The first day was a full introduction to the whole UK sales team of the complete service – every single bell and whistle was covered.

I sat in on the session for personal orientation, because the second day was my follow-up session, focused on creating tailored Sales Value Propositions.

The objective of my session was to translate all of the first day's technical knowledge and insights into a series of customer-centric positioning statements focused on the client's key strategic market sectors.

The interesting thing I noticed on Day One was that when the launch team were explaining the "Processes" and "People" elements of the offering, the sales team seemed to disengage somewhat. There was an atmosphere of "blah, blah, we've heard this all before, yawn, yawn."

However, I had already become impressed by the range of products, processes, and people that made up this new Managed Services offering. I interjected and made the point to everyone that I was the kind of businessman they needed to inspire.

I stressed their need to deal with a "familiarity breeding contempt" mindset. They had to begin to see things through the eyes of the customer. If they didn't, then the ultimate impact was going to be decidedly uninspiring.

They got the message, and the next day the sales teams worked together energetically and developed some excellent SVPs using the full range of their organisation's capabilities. The SVP process did an excellent job in getting everybody onto the same value-based page from the very first day of their Managed Services launch.

Differentiation because you know your competitors' position

> "By having a strong grasp on the competitive landscape, it is easier to effectively position yourself in different ways, including value propositions."
> —Mark Evans, *Forbes* contributor

I was working with a group of account managers from a major telecom client. The sales issue we were addressing was the need to differentiate your solutions from your competitor's solutions.

We had discussed a number of points, one of which was the need to be fully acquainted with the competitive solutions on offer. The key insight was that differentiation is situational and not generic. Uniqueness should always be a function of what is needed to satisfy the customer's requirements and an understanding of the scope of each competitor's solution – unique situation by unique situation.

One of the account managers then proceeded to present his solution, which highlighted a unique feature. In the ensuing feedback session, his colleagues started to harangue him about the validity of this unique feature. There were other suppliers that could offer this particular functionality, they said, so it was not a very good idea to highlight it as unique.

His response was to agree with them – in part. He said that they were correct about those competitors that could offer that same functionality. However, on this particular occasion, he told us that he knew he was not competing with those particular rivals. They could not offer the functionality, and so he felt quite confident about promoting the capability as unique – *in that specific situation.*

He was absolutely correct. There is real competitive advantage for those who utilise the competitor analyst's skills effectively and then boldly declare their differentiation.

Differentiation because you are tailoring your solution

"According to a 2014 study by Qvidian, salespeople often lose deals because they haven't customized their content to their buyer's needs."
—Leyl Black, Head of Communications at One Medical Group

In our original example below, you see how we are presenting our solution as a tailored package, in order to stand out and be perceived as different.

"Combining our proprietary digital technology with our experienced sales team, we will contact each customer quarterly about special offers and the financial benefits of contract renewal."

We are combining our technology product with our experienced sales team and presenting a broader-based, bespoke approach to address the customer's pain, its effects, and its costs.

We've underpinned our differentiation by adding the word "proprietary" to our digital technology product – meaning something that is used, produced, or marketed under *exclusive* legal right of the inventor or maker.

I recall one sales team that had just completed the 4 Ps exercise and was beginning to identify Unique Selling Points (USP) and Points of Differentiation (POD). They had found some differentiators among the overall lists of capabilities they had just compiled, but they were not satisfied that they had found enough "stand out from the crowd" qualities, so they started to discuss additional ideas that might just add some extra "bite" to their SVPs.

They soon realised that the complete 4 Ps exercise revealed a huge differentiator: their competitors could not emulate the overall range of value-adding capabilities that they had available to them.

The second insight they came up with was derived directly from the first. They saw that most of their organisation's capabilities were neither USPs nor PODs; however, when some were connected together into a genuine tailored solution, it became a unique offering.

They had discovered the meaning of synergy – and what's more, it would differentiate their offering from their competitors.

> "For any organisation today, differentiation that is wanted by the customer is more challenging than at any time in history, but it remains at the heart of successful marketing. More importantly, it remains the key to a company's survival."
> —Professor Malcolm McDonald, Value Propositions, 2016

It is quite amazing to me how little work is done in businesses as a whole – and specifically in the sales teams – regarding uniqueness and differentiation.

Usually, my workshops are the only time most salespeople can remember that there has been any kind of effort to:

- Identify the full range of organisational capabilities, i.e. the 4 Ps
- Highlight the capabilities that are unique or different from competitor offerings

So let's take a look at what might be a Unique Selling Point (USP) or a Point of Differentiation (POD) in your organisation.

So, What Is a USP?

A USP could be thought of as "what you have that competitors don't" (WhatIs.com).

Listed below are different ways I've seen of highlighting USPs in an SVP. Remember, they have to be *genuine* USPs, and not just wishful thinking!

Feel free to adjust the wording or fill in the blanks to suit your particular need.

- "We are the only … "
- "Our exclusive relationship with … "
- "A fully customised vehicle for … "
- "We have the sole agency for … "
- "Our proprietary technology … "

- "We deliver an award-winning service … "
- "We provide a bespoke solution … "
- "Our market-leading position … "
- "We are the single provider of … "
- "We provide a unique process … "
- "Producing unrivalled test performance"
- "The best Health and Safety record in the sector"
- "The widest coverage in the UK"
- "The most service staff on call"

So, What Is a POD?

A POD could be thought of as "something we and our competitors do, but we demonstrate it in a clearly superior way."

Listed below are different ways I've seen of highlighting PODs in an SVP. Again, feel free to adjust the wording or fill in the blanks to suit your particular need.

- "Faster than … "
- "Slower than … "
- "Wider coverage of … "
- "More service agents on call"
- "Less expensive than … "
- "Open longer than … "
- "More localised representation"
- "Greater global presence"
- "A cleaner carbon footprint"
- "Higher level of accreditation than … "

The lists are not considered comprehensive. There are probably a lot more examples; I just have not encountered them yet!

Before you choose your specific USP or POD, there are two underlying principles to consider:

- Differentiators are situational. As sales situations change, so do differentiators. What is unique today may well not be unique tomorrow. Every situation is unique.

- USPs and PODS need to be completely relevant and add clear business value to the customer situation you are confronting. "Spraying and praying" is not a good idea!

Now it's your turn.
Go back to your solution and reassess its description:

- Does it draw on the 4 Ps?
- Is it a tailored solution?
- Have you reviewed the USP and POD listings?
- Which description applies to your solution as either a unique feature or a genuine differentiator?

Upgrade your solution to a *differentiated* solution.
My differentiated solution is:

_____

_____

_____

CHAPTER SEVEN

Stage Four – Return on Investment (ROI)

———◆———

> "Only 5 percent of companies have financially quantified Value Propositions, and developing them will differentiate your company."
> —Professor Malcolm McDonald and Grant Oliver

The third and final question we need to answer is:

What's in it for me? What is the financial payoff?

So what measurable value does your customer get in return for investing in your products and services?

It's important to note that whatever ROI we will deliver needs to connect back to the cost factor at Stage One.

Without an accurate cost calculation in place, there is no benchmark economic value from which the customer can assess a monetary return from using our differentiated solution. This is a critical step, as it drives a powerful value-for-money narrative and can definitely reduce the pressure on price.

Without the cost metrics, organisations and Account Managers have little choice but to default to qualitative ROI statements such as "increased productivity," "enhanced efficiency," or "improved customer experience."

Doesn't everybody say that anyway? As statements go, they appear to say a lot; actually they say very little.

You are in danger here of diminishing all the good work you've done up to this point. You have a clear definition of the customer's situation and a well-defined differentiated solution to fix the problem. But you have no measurable ROI.

It was all going so well! Why are we reluctant to commit to a monetary ROI? Here are some reasons I have personally encountered:

- We have not developed a well defined pain, impact, and cost statement for the customer situation.
- There is no financial track record of how our solution has performed with other customers experiencing similar issues.
- Companies are simply not prepared to "put their money where their mouth is" as far as the performance of their products and services is concerned.

I need to stress here that I am not advocating that we make irresponsible claims of customer advantages and benefits, including financial returns that are neither realistic nor supportable.

However, in my experience, if we have engaged in effective consulting around the customer's pain, impact, and cost, then we are in a much stronger position to assess the measurable value we can deliver.

In our original example, we had a very clear calculation of the falling customer retention index, the number of actual customers lost over the period and the average contract size. From that well-researched data, we were able to estimate that lost sales had cost the customer around £200,000 of revenue over the period. We also knew what the cause was: no customer contact at all during the contract period.

So what ROI do we believe we will provide the customer when our proprietary digital technology and our experienced sales team are brought into play? What payback will we generate when customers are contacted each quarter about special offers and the financial benefits of contract renewal?

It so happens that we do have a proven track record of quantifiable success for this solution, and on that basis we are prepared to commit to an ROI.

Remember, this is the SVP – the trailer, not the movie. We will address all the important issues related to the implementation of our solution once we have the customer's undivided attention.

We want a legitimate ROI to impact the customer's thinking and give us some decisive competitive advantage. We may not be closing the deal here, however we are looking to decisively move ourselves to the front of the line and put our competitors on the back foot.

"The very act of financially quantifying the benefits, even if they are standard benefits, will give you an advantage over your competitors."
—Professor Malcolm McDonald, Value Propositions, 2016

Let's take a look at what that ROI commitment might look like in our example SVP:

"We agreed earlier that your retention rates have fallen for the past three years from 90 percent to the current level of 80 percent, due to a complete lack of contact with customers over the period of their annual contract.

"This means that over that same period your business has lost about 500 customers. With an average customer spend of £450 each year; around £200,000 of revenue has been lost.

"Combining our proprietary digital technology with our experienced sales team, we will contact each customer quarterly about special offers and the financial benefits of contract renewal.

"We will reduce the number of customer defections by at least 50 percent over the three-year period, which will produce revenue of around £110,000."

So why did we choose 50 percent reduction in customer defections? Why not 75 percent or even 100 percent?

As you will see in the fifth and final stage of the SVP structure, we know from other similar implementations that we have regularly achieved a 60 percent reduction in customer defections. So we have good reason to be confident in setting the customer's expectations, whilst being prudent with our ROI commitment.

One of the most memorable examples of the power of quantifying the customer's ROI was an Account Manager who was pitching to a legal practice for a piece of expensive office hardware. The opportunity was competitive and there was a pressing need for the Account Manager to find a way of presenting a differentiated solution that stood out from the other potential suppliers'.

In the workshop, her group developed an SVP based on the information she had. However, the exercise showed that there was still some outstanding information needed before the SVP was in good shape, including solid metrics and a measurable customer ROI.

At a workshop review a couple months later, I followed up with the group their experiences of using SVPs. Our Account Manager told us a very interesting story.

Following the original workshop, she had gathered the outstanding information and polished the SVP. As it was a formal pitch to a senior partner in the legal practice, she had rehearsed her pitch and the SVP in particular, until she became comfortable with the narrative.

However, just in case she lost track, she had a hard copy

of the SVP resting on the keyboard of the laptop that she was using for the pitch.

At the opportune moment, she glanced down to collect her thoughts and her client saw her.

"What are you looking at?" the client asked.

"Some notes," she said.

"Let me see!" the client said.

Our Account Manager showed her the paper containing the SVP.

She read it and then declared, "I want that!"

Her finger was pointing at one particular line. She was pointing at the ROI!

The deal was done then and there.

CHAPTER EIGHT

Stage Five – Anecdotal Evidence

An important factor to bear in mind when promoting or pitching solutions is the mindset of the decision-maker or key influencer to whom we are presenting the SVP.

No matter how great a job we've done up until now, a new prospect or a lapsed customer will always have some sense of potential risk in their minds.

"Am I making the right choice?"

"Can I trust this organisation to perform in line with what they've told me?"

"Will their impressive solution really deliver the results they are claiming?"

Authentic testimonials and case studies reduce the fear of the unknown in people's mind. Clear evidence will create credibility and confidence for customers to say "Yes" to doing business with us.

"Customers love it when you make it clear that
you can deliver. So tell them: 'We can do that'
and give them some brief proofs or examples."
—Robert Craven, the FD Centre

Conciseness, though, is still the order of the day. We simply haven't got the time to indulge in full-blown testimonials and three pages of case study within the structure of an SVP.

There will be plenty of opportunity to unwrap a more expansive testimonial or case study later. Right now, we simply need to assure the customer of our ability to deliver an effective solution.

We're going to provide that assurance using three key factors:

1. The Name of the Customer

You need to identify the customer, the subject of the story, wherever possible. Your story has to be real and relevant. If identifying the customer is not possible, then you will need to position your success story in the same market sector as your current customer.

2. Same Pain or Same Solution

Ensure the business pain or the actual solution at the heart of your message is identical or very similar to the one you are addressing for your customer or prospect. Again, relevance is vital.

3. Return on Investment

Quantify the payoff that the customer received by doing business with you. There needs to be some measurable business value, the all-important "what's in it for them." If you haven't a monetary value available, then try to be as specific as you can about the quality of the business outcome.

So here's our example SVP with the final stage, our anecdote, inserted:

> "We agreed earlier that your retention rates have fallen for the past three years from 90 percent to the current level of 80 percent, due to a complete lack of contact with customers over the period of their annual contract.

"This means that over that same period your business has lost about 500 customers. With an average customer spend of £450 each year; around £200,000 of revenue has been lost.

"Combining our proprietary digital technology with our experienced sales team, we will contact each customer quarterly about special offers and the financial benefits of contract renewal.

"We will reduce the number of customer defections by at least 50 percent over the three-year period, which will produce revenue of around £110,000.

"ClearCut Limited is currently using our technology, reducing customer turnover by around 60 percent and achieving incremental revenue of £85,000."

Timed at around forty-three seconds, we're near the top end of the SVP time frame.

My anecdote is:

1. Name of customer: _____

2. Describe the similar problem or similar solution:

_____

_____

_____

3. Return on Investment: _____

_____

_____

Now you can:

- connect the five elements of your SVP together to form one complete positioning statement;
- check your timing with a colleague – the whole SVP

needs to run between 30–45 seconds;
- wordsmith the content, "iron out the wrinkles," and edit out unnecessary words or phrases – if you've over-run the time, be brutal;
- edit it again if necessary to improve the flow and the timing.

"As long as you don't prove your claims, people are unlikely to really believe them. And your value proposition becomes useless."
—Kissmetrics Blog

One more thing …

I am often asked what my thoughts are about SVP-related information that is difficult to obtain or seemingly out of reach; it's usually the metrics, the costs of the pain, and the ROI that we can deliver.

My advice is to go after key information with skill and determination and not give up until you have exhausted all your options. Don't be lazy and don't take an "it'll do" approach; that's not the way that professional salespeople behave.

Any missing information will diminish your SVP's effectiveness; it will be less compelling and less impactful as a consequence.

However, if you've gone as far as you can, you have probably gone much further than your competitors, building a clearer picture of the customer's situation and developing a powerfully differentiated solution.

You have also set in place a broader, value-based narrative that does not need to have the price and discounts as its main features. Your SVP may not be complete, however it could still be an effective enough trailer that your customer will want to invest quality time watching your movie!

"The quickest way to make a lasting negative impression is to waste someone's time; use it cavalierly or take up more of it than you need. If you don't have something to say, don't set up a meeting just to make contact. A contact that is really worth having will respond to your 'I just wanted to meet you' by making sure you never meet again."
—Mark McCormack, *What They Don't Teach You at Harvard Business School*

CHAPTER NINE

The Versatility of Sales Value Propositions

"The need to sell more than the product requires an enormous change in emphasis in most companies … the traditional sales force that sold just the product is going to be at a distinct disadvantage."
—John Rock, *Key Account Management*

SVPs are extremely versatile and can make a considerable contribution to a wide range of sales and marketing initiatives.

Across the whole marketing and sales environment, there is hardly a situation where a well presented SVP cannot play an extraordinarily productive role.

In this chapter, we'll examine various sales and marketing settings in which an SVP will make your message to customers and prospects far more resilient and far more persuasive.

Most salespeople who already have some understanding

of the role of SVPs tend to see that role as being primarily related to progressing sales opportunities.

While an SVP has an important role to play in pursuing and winning a sales opportunity, we also need to highlight its role in positioning and communicating unique business value in other equally important sales and marketing spheres.

As we change perspective there are some important points to remember:

1. The SVP structure remains constant regardless of the sales perspective we take.
2. The timing of thirty to forty-five seconds continues to be the guideline that determines conciseness.
3. The "one pain per SVP" discipline is unchanged. If we need to address more than one pain, then we will need more than one SVP.
4. The Stage One pain, impact, cost statement remains at 40–45 percent of the total SVP; the customer-centric focus remains paramount.
5. The various metrics, although sometimes challenging, should still be aggressively pursued and included wherever possible.

Note: The example SVP at each of the following levels will only focus on Stage One, the pain, impact, and cost statement. In my experience, this is not only the most pivotal part of the SVP but usually the toughest to research and create.

For a refresher on the development of the four remaining stages, please revisit Chapters 5-8.

Company Level

> "It turns out that many businesses don't succeed because they have weak value propositions."
> —David Khim, Sumo.com

An organisation's primary objective for utilizing a company-level SVP is to send a powerful message of unique business value and proven expertise to its complete marketplace. Company SVPs concentrate on single, high-level, high-priority business issues impacting most, if not all, of its customers and prospects.

The business issues are those it believes it can address with proven expertise and a successful track record.

The SVP describes the specific pain, the typical operational impact, and the typical cost effecting those customers and prospects in its market space.

The term "typical impact and cost" is used at this high level as a kind of benchmark. The benchmark is usually attached to a mid-range-size customer or prospect, from which other organisations can scale the level of impact and cost as it relates to their business situation.

The Company level SVP describes succinctly how a tailored solution delivers differentiated and measurable business value in resolving that high-level business pain, and its typical impact and cost.

The measurable ROI will reference the solution's performance, again using a typical mid-range customer where there is likely to be accurate metrics and anecdotal evidence of the solution's effectiveness. Other organisations of differing sizes can then scale their own potential ROI accordingly.

The process of developing a finely tuned Company SVP can be challenging. Gaining consensus at each of the five SVP stages from a representative group of individuals is, as you can imagine, quite testing! It is a highly iterative process of research, testing, wordsmithing, and refinement.

However, in my experience, fortune favours the brave!

In our pain, impact, and cost example below, the actual metric highlighting the cost, i.e. the lost sales, was obtained from legitimate market research carried out by a third party. You will also see that the pain and impact section is not written as a "problem with consequences" statement but in a more "opportunity with payoffs" style.

Either method can work for you – it's a judgement call, based on the specific situation you are facing.

> "The real-time availability of mission-critical information enables public and private sector organisations to speed up their decision-making processes, boost the customer experience, and create decisive competitive advantage.
>
> "Research shows that in the retail sector alone, a poor customer experience costs UK brands £234 billion a year in lost sales."

One of the more rewarding outputs is not just the actual SVP itself but a far more outward-looking attitude from everybody actively involved in the process, and a more precise and more confident view of their organisation's unique position in its marketplace.

A Sales Director told me that he had observed a definite upgrade in the level of customer interaction across his whole sales team: better questioning, improved consulting skills, and much stronger customer focus in meetings.

He was in no doubt that the upgrade in skill was a direct consequence of each team member's active involvement in the development of the Company and Segment level SVPs.

So where would you look to use a Company level SVP?

- Company website
- PR and advertising materials and activities
- Press releases
- Prospecting activities in new markets and with new prospects
- Formal business presentations
- Induction of new employees
- Company annual report/Chairman's statement
- Potential investors and shareholders

- Executive summary of a formal business proposal
- Creating a strategic positioning theme for other levels of SVPs

---

"When I reviewed a bunch of websites, the conclusion was that a missing or poor value proposition is one of the most common shortcomings."
—Peep Laja, CEO and founder of CXL Institute

Segment Level

The Segment level SVP is where I have seen a lot of client activity in recent years. Sales organisations that have a multi-sector business strategy are seeing a clear need to review the thrust of their market positioning and messaging as never before.

The focus is now noticeably moving towards a more customer-centric message, with a strong emphasis on measurable value, differentiation, and proven segment expertise.

This movement has to do with two major market forces:

- Strong customer pressure for suppliers to provide a clearer and more precise value-based narrative
- Unprecedented levels of competition and the need to make a clear break from the "Me Too" syndrome

SVPs play a very effective role in dealing with these two issues head-on.

Two of my clients in the high-tech and manufacturing sectors have invested time and resources creating Company- and Segment-level SVPs to support their sector strategies in European and UK markets.

In one case, the sales and marketing teams worked together over a two-day period, creating six segment SVPs to support the organisation's pan-European sector-focused sales strategy.

There are some parallels in the way that Segment level and Company level SVPs are created, because of the larger audiences the two SVP types are targeting.

The key differences are:

- There is frequently more than one segment that an organisation has on its strategic planning radar. Unlike the Company level, there is more than one audience population.
- There may be more than one pain in each segment, which it believes it can address with proven expertise and a successful track record.

This means there will be more than one SVP per segment and multiple SVPs across the complete segments strategy, depending on the numbers of segments and number of issues it believes it can address effectively.

Some clients find that creating this number of SVPs is somewhat daunting, given the challenge of creating just one Company SVP!

However, it is important to reflect on what this position actually means. It demonstrates that there are a number of very clear opportunities to develop a broader base of credibility and recognition across a wide range of audiences – prospects and customers. That's got to be good news!

There are also some real frontline sales benefits that emerge by creating a range of Segment level SVPs:

Building Confidence and Focus Across Your Team

The "roll-up" impact produced by each of the multiple-segment SVPs becomes impressive. The overall effect on the sales team and other roles within the organisation becomes much higher, boosting confidence and focusing the sales and marketing mindset.

One Managing Director told me that she was seeing a much higher quality of sales discussion in conversations and meetings with her Account Managers, as a direct result of working with the SVP creation process.

Opening the Sales Conversation

Segment SVPs provide frontline salespeople with an excellent positioning statement when opening conversations with new prospects.

From the start they have, at their fingertips, compelling Segment SVPs that they can use, quickly and effectively, to build credibility by positioning their organisation's expertise and track record in that prospect's marketplace.

Expanding the Sales Pipeline

Multiple segments with accompanying SVPs also provide salespeople with a clear pathway to expand their sales meetings with customers and prospects alike.

They are able, with greater confidence, to create a broader conversation across more potential segment issues, using the SVPs as leverage.

"To fix your messengers, fix your message."
—Harry Beckwith, *Selling the Invisible*

The construction of the five-stage SVP is identical to the Company level SVP.

The starting point, as always, is the selection of the various pains that the organisation can address in each sector. Proven expertise and a successful track record are again important factors in the selection process.

Here's a pain, impact, cost example from the logistics sector:

"Inefficient supply chain practices can lead to errors in the warehouse that have a direct impact on efficiency, costs, and profitability. For example, incorrect location of goods, incorrect picking, and shipping all add up to a typical industry cost of between £40 and £200 per incorrect item delivered."

From this point, we can work our way through the remaining four stages of the SVP structure as I detailed them in Chapters Five- Eight.

So where would you look to use a Segment level SVP?

- Company website
- Company newsletter/magazine
- Segment-related PR and advertising materials
- Segment case studies/testimonials
- Specialist exhibitions and trade shows
- Press releases in specialist trade magazines
- Segment-focused product launches
- Prospecting activities in new segment markets and new prospects
- Customer meetings
- Formal business presentations to a specific segment audience
- Executive summary of a formal business proposal
- Creating a consistent positioning theme for other SVP types.

One more thing …

Segmentation can take other forms than simply dividing up the marketplace by sector type, although this is the most prevalent method. Another model I've seen is segmentation by an organisation's own product group or business solutions. In simple terms, the business strategy is driven by solution or product group, as opposed to addressing specific customer business needs or issues in designated market sectors.

Creating SVPs to support this kind of "solution-based" segmentation strategy can be still handled by the five-stage structure. However, to ensure that the SVP maintains integrity, we have to take one step back, because with a solution-based segmentation, our starting point is actually Stage Two of the SVP structure.

The question we have to answer first is, "If this is an effective solution, then what are the pain, the impact, and the cost that it resolves?"

We have to go back and define Stage One first, before we can make our way through the other stages and complete the SVP.

Interestingly, this is the approach that worked successfully for our innovative business banker on pages 16–18.

Customer Level

> "Partnering has to be more than a philosophy; it has to be tangible, transparent, structured, and measurable."
> —George March, CEO, Galliford plc

The Customer level is the point at which we need to become far more precise in our SVP targeting and content.

Unlike the Company and Segment level, where we are focused on a relatively large population of customers and prospects, the Customer level concentrates on a single intact business or a single business unit within a more complex organisation.

The sales objective here is building and sustaining a long-term relationship with a customer or prospect because we have identified clear business development opportunities based on a value-based partnership.

To build an effective partnership-based SVP requires a certain quality of information around which the five stages can be developed.

So what do we need to know?

The *customer's goal or vision* is a good place to start, as it describes where the customer is heading in terms of its business growth, market position, and brand development over the next three–five years or so.

> "A goal is a statement of a desired future an organization wishes to achieve. It describes what the organization is trying accomplish."
> —Cothran and Wysocki, University of Florida

Goal statements will typically focus on any number of "desired futures," such as:

- Their competitive position: "become undisputed market leader"
- Their market coverage: "become an established global business"
- Their range of products/services: "become an end-to-end solution provider"
- Their customer service: "become the recognised supplier of choice"

We need to identify the customer's goal, which will exist either as a formalised statement or will be confirmed more informally by key individuals.

To realise its goal, an organisation will set itself a number of short-to-medium-term objectives that it needs to accomplish. These objectives act as milestones and enable the organisation to make and measure progress towards its goal, step by step.

This is where we should start to see a clearer role for ourselves in supporting the customer to reach some of these objectives. We need to remember that our SVP is going to embrace the goal and connect to appropriate objectives in a specific and concise fashion.

As an example:

> "You confirmed that a major step towards becoming the leader in the regional newspaper market is by increasing weekly circulation from 150,000 to 200,000 readers by 31 December 2019; and by creating 75 additional retail distribution points, plus new sales from hotels, regional transportation hubs, and health centres, increasing revenue by £300,000 per annum."

You can see from the Stage One statement that you know:

1. The goal: "leader in the regional newspaper market"

2. Three shorter-term objectives:
   • Additional retail distribution points
   • New income from three additional sales points
   • Revenue increase of £300,000

A Customer level SVP will need to describe briefly how a tailored business solution will deliver differentiated and measurable business value by assisting the customer to achieve the three shorter-term objectives, wherever possible, and make progress towards their goal of market leadership.

Let's bear in mind that the SVP is the trailer, not the movie, so the solution description will still need to be brief and to the point. It's very easy right here to spend too much time in too much detail; it's important to spend a little time polishing for brevity!

Remember, our intention is to instigate initial partnering credibility by communicating a well-crafted positioning statement that covers the shorter-term objectives and, most important, the longer-term goal.

So where would you look to use a Customer level SVP?

• Case studies/testimonials
• Relevant product launch
• Customer meetings
• Meeting agenda
• Customer meeting, follow-up communication
• Formal business presentations
• Executive summary of a formal business proposal

"In order of importance, respondents rated the relationship-based approach, value delivered, and product and service performance as the elements they most value in salespeople/supplier relationships. Interestingly … price and cost savings were lower down the list."
—TACK International, Buyers' View of Salespeople, 2012

Opportunity Level

The Opportunity level is another key point at which we are far more precise in our SVP targeting and content.

Opportunity SVPs focus on a specific business pain that impacts the operational performance of a customer or a prospect.

Opportunity-level SVPs describe how a tailored business solution delivers differentiated and measurable business value, enabling the customer or prospect to resolve the specific issue and its operational impact.

We covered development of an Opportunity level SVP in detail and stage by stage in Chapters Four-Eight.

> **"As part of the sales process, buyers expect to hear how sellers' products or services will materially contribute to the buying organization's success – and why the seller is uniquely qualified to deliver that value."**
> **—Barbara Bix, Accounting Web**

One more thing …

Proactively creating opportunities is a very effective way of building a sales pipeline. It has been accepted for some time that these types of sales opportunities, successfully pursued, have a significantly higher bid: win ratio than the traditional "react to a customer invitation" type of opportunity.

It is, though, a more demanding process when it comes to building the business case and getting the customer's buy-in. You are asking them to prioritise and invest in resolving a business issue that is not yet on their radar as a priority project.

Care has to be taken with this kind of situation, regardless of its legitimacy. If you present the business case carelessly, the customer's view will be that you are only trying to find a way to sell them more stuff!

An SVP approach, though, is a very effective way to work through your business case in a customer-centric fashion.

The Stage One pain, impact, and cost statement that you will have to develop needs to convince *you* first, that there is genuine, measurable value that can be delivered to the customer.

A good idea is to test that Stage One statement with a colleague – if they're not convinced, you're going to have very little chance with your customer. However, if it resonates then go ahead and develop your full SVP and use it as leverage to get the opportunity onto your customer's radar.

> "A winning executive creates the conditions of victory before taking any initiative. A losing executive takes initiative before knowing how to succeed."
> —Donald Krause, The Art of War for Executives

Individual Level

> "The very best salespeople engineer alignment with personal agendas and corporate drivers."
> —Tony J. Hughes, smamasterminds.com

Individual SVPs focus on how a specific business pain impacts the personal effectiveness and job performance of an individual in a customer or prospect's organisation. In order to gain maximum leverage from the Individual SVP, the person is going to be either a confirmed decision-maker or a confirmed decision-influencer.

The objective of the SVP would be to express unique business and *personal* value, and as a consequence secure a decisive level of support from that individual. Care needs to be taken in how the SVP is developed and shaped, given the very personal nature of the issues involved.

My own recommendation is that when an Individual SVP is needed, the personalised emphasis at Stage One should be on the impact element. Any kind of cost should only be integrated into the SVP if the individual has willingly disclosed monetarized metrics like salary, bonuses, personal Key Performance Indicators (KPIs), and job objectives.

The impact elements can normally be narrowed down to three key factors that the business pain could directly affect:

1. The ability to achieve primary job objectives and KPIs
2. How the individual is rewarded
3. The individual's ultimate job security

As you can see from the example below, Individual level SVPs describe how the tailored business solution delivers not only differentiated and measurable business value but also enable the individual to achieve specific job objectives.

You can also see how the original Opportunity-level SVP has been adjusted to accommodate the personalised content.

> "We agreed that customer retention rates have fallen for the past three years from 90 percent to the current level of 80 percent. With an average annual customer spend of £450, it is estimated that around £200,000 of revenue has been lost. *As a result, you have not been able to achieve your sales objectives or recruit staff and have had to apply severe cuts in your departmental expenditure.*
>
> "Combining our proprietary digital technology with our experienced sales team, we will contact customers quarterly about special offers and the financial benefits of contract renewal.
>
> "We will reduce customer defections by 50 percent over a two-year period, producing revenue of around £110,000, *enabling you and the business to achieve sales objectives.*
>
> "ClearCut Limited uses our technology and

has reduced customer turnover by 60 percent and achieved incremental revenue of £85,000."

So where would you look to use an Individual level SVP?

- Formal/informal one-to-one meetings with key individuals
- Follow up email/letter to key individuals
- Formal presentations to a role-specific audience
- Articles/press releases focusing on role-specific readers

CHAPTER TEN

Tales of Success

————◆————

"Carpe Diem!"

> "The minute he read out the SVP, the majority of the audience sat up in their seats and I knew we had their attention. Most important, we had the business!"

The majority of my client work involves real, "live" sales situations. Whatever the reason for my engagement, I always ask that the marketplace is brought into the meeting, coaching session, or training event. Nothing helps the theory along more effectively than reality!

Occasionally, when that work spreads into a longer period of time, you get to track some of the more important sales opportunities from their inception to their completion.

In one such situation, my client was asked to submit a proposal in support of a major European bank's initiative to market their products and services more effectively to their customer base, spread across six hundred branches.

The selection process was in two phases. The first phase was an initial proposal, from which three potential suppliers would be shortlisted to provide a fuller, more comprehensive proposal, from which the final decision would be made.

We were just starting to run a series of the one-day SVP workshops when this proposal request appeared. The client's Sales Director and Sales Manager had taken direct responsibility for the proposal because of its importance to the business.

They asked if an SVP could be produced in one of the workshops, to support their initial bid to get onto the short list. We did just that and they were shortlisted.

Shortly after, we began to run a series of consulting skills workshops, and from time to time the bank proposal would be the centre of attention once again, as the Sales Director and Sales Manager prepared their final pitch: a formal presentation to the senior management team at the bank's HQ.

Just ahead of the formal client presentation, the Sales Manager approached me with an idea and asked, "We are planning to introduce our pitch by using the SVP; it'll be the first slide they see and we believe it will grab their attention. What do you think?"

I reflected on everything we had covered and discussed in the various workshops. It was time to put our money where our mouths were. "A great idea," I said. "I believe it will work!"

We polished the SVP one more time and I waited for the feedback from the presentation.

The Sales Manager told us later that he was observing the client group as the Sales Director made the pitch. He said, "The minute he read out the SVP, the majority of the audience sat up in their seats and I knew we had their attention. Most important, we had the business!"

Know Your Enemy

> "There is real competitive advantage for those who
> utilise the competitor analyst's skills effectively and
> then boldly declare their differentiation."

I was working with a group of account managers from a major telecom client. One of the major sales issues we were addressing was the need to differentiate your solutions from your competitor's solutions.

We had discussed a number of points, among which was the need to be fully acquainted with the customer's requirements, but also with the corresponding competitive solutions being offered.

The key point was that differentiation is situational and not generic. Uniqueness should be a function of what is needed to satisfy a specific customer's requirements, and an understanding of the actual scope of each competitor's capabilities – unique situation by unique situation.

One of the account managers then proceeded to present his solution, which highlighted a unique feature. In the ensuing feedback session, his colleagues started to harangue him about the validity of this unique feature. There were other suppliers that could offer this particular functionality, they said, so it was not correct to highlight it as unique.

His response was to agree with them – in part. He said that they were correct about those competitors that could offer that same functionality. However, he went on to say that, on this particular occasion, he was not competing with those particular rivals.

The companies he was now competing with could not offer that functionality, and so he felt quite within his rights to promote that capability as unique – in that specific situation.

"We have a great movie, but a lousy trailer!"

> "His reaction when he and the team had fine-tuned their tailored SVP was, "This is absolutely what we needed, perfect!"

More and more UK public sector speciality services are looking to market their services outside their own regional organisations and operate more like private-sector businesses.

One such organisation was a local authority recruitment department, responsible for all forms of recruitment across their own local authority, now looking to branch out and offer its services to other local authorities.

Four of the team, including the General Manager, attended one of my one-day workshops, along with representatives of other speciality services. The General Manager, in his introduction, gave us an overview of a major marketing project that he and the team had put together. The project was aimed at marketing his group's recruitment services to about twelve or so other local authorities spread across central and southern UK.

They had put together an impressive plan, creating a brochure that introduced the team, providing an overview of their services and track record. They had even started planning a road show to follow up the mailing.

The General Manager told us that despite all the planning, though, he had concerns. He explained that the kinds of individuals that he was trying to reach were very busy people with other priorities; the project needed an attention-grabbing message to get onto their radar.

The team worked with the SVP process and then put its principles to work on creating an SVP to support their initiative. To say the General Manager was excited with the result would be an understatement. His reaction when he and the team had fine-tuned their tailored SVP was, "This is absolutely what we needed, perfect!"

Getting to the Front of the Line

> "The Account Manager was convinced that the SVP's precise, tailored messaging had made a decisive contribution in capturing the customer's attention."

Remember the Account Manager from Chapter One who attended my one-day "Communicating Unique Business

Value" workshop? He had a solid business solution to a particular customer's business issue and no obvious competition – but every time he met with the business principal, their meeting was constantly interrupted.

He had done everything he could to make their meetings successful and had become quite frustrated. In an attempt to deal with the challenge, the group helped him develop a very polished SVP and some creative ideas of how he could use it with the customer.

The Account Manager inserted the SVP created in the workshop at the top of the customer's next meeting agenda, as a kind of mission statement. When he called the customer later to confirm the meeting, the customer told him that their meeting would be at the warehouse, because "we'll get some peace and quiet there." The result was a very productive meeting.

The SVP's precise, tailored messaging had made a decisive contribution in capturing the customer's attention, leading to a far more effective meeting and ultimately a successful sales outcome.

The Power of the ROI

> "She read it and then declared 'I want that!' Her finger was pointing at one particular line. She was pointing at the ROI! The deal was done then and there."

Remember our Account Manager who was pitching to a legal practice for a piece of expensive office hardware? The opportunity was competitive and the Account Manager was looking for a differentiated solution that stood out from the other potential suppliers.

In the workshop, her group developed an SVP. At a workshop review a couple of months later, our Account Manager told us that during her formal pitch, she had a hard copy of the SVP resting on the keyboard of her laptop.

Her client saw her glance at it and asked to see the paper, which contained the SVP.

She read it and then declared "I want that!" She was pointing at the ROI.

The deal was done then and there.

Making Appointments the Value-Based Way

> "He concluded his story by telling us how many of his initial telephone calls he had converted into face-to-face meetings – his strike rate was 100 percent!"

Remember the British bank that wanted to upgrade its selling to its business services consultants? When we regrouped to review the personal progress that each consultant had made in implementing some of the new sales approaches, one story made a big impression.

The consultant had been given the responsibility of introducing two new bank products to potential business prospects in his territory. He emphasized that these prospects were genuine new business targets and not current clients of the bank. In setting a meeting with each prospect, he fashioned tailored SVPs based on the business issues the two products were designed to address.

Once his prospect confirmed they had the business need, he then delivered his pre-designed SVP to secure a face-to-face meeting. His strike rate was 100 percent!

Changing the Conversation

> "The 'pain, impact, cost' exercise breathed new life into the price-pressured sales opportunity and a lot more confidence into the Account Manager."

Remember my client who was selling materials to a road surfacing company? The contractor had been using a cheaper competitor's product and, although the cheaper material had disappointed, my client was still under a lot of pressure from the contractor to reduce the price of higher-quality product.

In the workshop, the team worked through the "pain, impact, cost" process. They saw the true cost to the contractor of using poor materials and from that position demonstrated the true value of the superior materials:

"Utility reinstatements have a high level of failure, typically 60+ percent, caused by poor compaction. These failures result in rework costs, local authority fines, loss of productivity and loss of reputation with the client, together with disruption to the public."

Clarifying these impacts was significant, not only because they are the key credibility-builders, but because they started an all important value-based narrative, which can reduce significantly the focus on price.

This example is very interesting when it comes to the cost implications of a larger number of impacts. The 60+ percent failure rate told the Account Manager how many failures had occurred. The Account Manager knew the average rework cost for each failure was between £300 and £800 per repair.

Local authority penalties, any further repair failures, and disruptions to the community sometimes run into millions of pounds. The genuine loss of productivity relates to the new revenue-generating projects the contractors' personnel could be working on if they were not tied up with the rework. This is not so easy to quantify at first sight, however it is possible.

If the contractor's failure reflects badly on the ultimate local Authority customer and demeans its reputation, then the customer will likely show the contractor the exit door, along with all the revenue and profit – a huge cost.

Standing Out from the Crowd

"We needed to give our Account Managers a message, and the confidence, to be in front of a customer and competently explain why they should be considered over another brand.

"We saw the SVP as critical to differentiation in a saturated market. As we saw in the workshops, lots of companies provide 'the same products to the same customers at the same price.'

"While we were/are very active in the market, we felt we were seen as a me-too provider, versus a stand-alone company with a unique offering.

"As a sales team, we had a fairly typical focus – selling more products. At the salesperson level, some of our team were struggling to articulate our uniqueness and value over our competitors'.

"We needed to give them a message, and the confidence, to be in front of a customer and competently explain why they should be considered over another brand.

"The other challenge we faced was that the things we believed and espoused as our SVPs, while indeed unique to the market, were not necessarily seen as unique or beneficial by some customers.

"We tried multiple times to create an SVP internally but kept coming back to what we believed, not necessarily what was of value to the customer.

"We needed our thinking challenged to help us address the feedback from the market and help to extract what our true value to the market really is."

"You know, but does your customer know that you know?"

"The winning bid was not based on a superior product; it was based on demonstrating a superior insight of the customer's priorities."

Remember the Sales Director who clarified the importance of aligning with the client's priorities first? His client, a big insurance brokerage, shared the client with their major competitor. Every time they attempted to win all of the business, the Managing Partner simply said "I need to keep you both on your toes."

They then received a Request for Proposal from the client, asking them to submit a proposal for all of the brokerage's business. Their proposal was rejected in favour of their prime competitor

They asked if they could discuss why they had lost the bid. They were told that their offering did not to cover a particular process, whereas the competitor had specifically highlighted this process in their proposal.

Though they also had that feature in their proposal, it was on a page quite near the end of the document. The client's response was "We didn't get that far!"

The winning bid was not based on a superior product; it was based on demonstrating a superior insight of the customer's priorities.

Playing with a Full Deck

> "They needed to deal with their *familiarity breeding contempt'* mindset … if they didn't, then the ultimate impact was going to be decidedly uninspiring."

Remember the global tech company that I told, in the workshop, that I was the kind of businessman they needed to inspire?

I had become impressed by the range of products, processes and people that made up this new Managed Services offering.

However, there was an atmosphere in the sales team of "blah, blah, we've heard this all before, yawn, yawn".

I could see that they had to begin to see things through the eyes of the customer. I stressed their need to deal with a "familiarity breeding contempt" mindset.

The next day, the sales teams worked together energetically and developed some excellent SVPs by using the full range of their organisation's Managed Services capabilities.

Mountaintops and Foothills

"Our account manager had gone beyond the quality of the SVP and used its structure as a way of assessing the status and health of the sales opportunity itself."

In workshop, I was working with a group of account managers from a major telecoms company. We were at the stage where we were creating SVPs using the live sales situations the group had brought to the workshop.

At the end of the day, I asked each member of the group for feedback on their major learnings. The feedback was very positive overall, but one account manager's response in particular was memorable.

We had used his "live" customer situation in the practice session, and the SVP his group had produced was above average. However, he was somewhat concerned that the SVP lacked a certain persuasive quality, due to missing customer information.

His feedback was different than the rest of the group's: "I have to go back to my customer and find different people to talk to and ask them different questions."

There was nothing wrong with his interpersonal skills. His lack of effectiveness was all about his peripheral vision. He was in the foothills, and he realised that he needed to "climb higher" and apply those skills more strategically.

For him, the SVP process had shown him that the Sales Strategist's mindset needed to kick in if he was to succeed.

So what were some of the things he needed to check out?

- Do I really know how my customer defines and measures success for this project?
- Am I talking to the right people?

- Am I asking the right questions?
- How will I truly differentiate myself?

Interestingly, our account manager had also said he needed to talk to different people. Who were they? They were probably the individuals who controlled or who had some influence over the customer's strategic decision-making process.

Our account manager had gone beyond the quality of the SVP and used its structure as a way of assessing the status and health of the sales opportunity itself.

CHAPTER ELEVEN

One More Thing …

---◆---

> "The growing disconnect between what the
> buyer wants and what the sales rep provides
> contributes to the systematic failure of providing
> real added value to the customer."
> —Qvidian's 2015 State of Sales Execution Report

Everything we've covered in this book has focused on the customer centricity of the five-stage SVP process. We know that the pain, impact, and cost statement has to drive the whole structure or it will almost certainly miss the mark.

Even when we started with the solution, we had to take a step back and ask the question, "If that's the solution, then what are the pain, impact, and cost that it resolves?"

However, salespeople and sales managers have also told me that the five-stage process provides them with an *internally focused* structure, which they use as a step-by-step approach to checking the "vital signs" of current sales opportunities.

Sales Managers say they review and coach their team using each of the five stages, to assess the customer business case being built and review the level of competitive advantage. Salespeople tell me they use the five-stage structure to self-assess opportunities or partner with colleagues to peer-coach each other.

I always refer to the afternoon session of the one-day workshop, which is devoted to presenting and critiquing SVPs as a "takeaway" process, because it can be easily replicated as part of any organisation's pipeline review. The forty-five-second SVP time frame also makes the process an excellent use of time.

The five-stage "health check" below will help you kick-start a review of your current sales opportunities – quickly and effectively.

SVP Stage	Question
Pain, impact, and cost	Is the customer's business situation defined accurately?
	Have we confirmed that business situation with the key individuals?
	Do we have monetary costs identified?
Solution	Does our solution fix the pain, impact, and cost?
	Have we considered our full range of capabilities?
	Have we tailored our solution?
Differentiation	Have we assessed our competitors' position?
	Have we identified their solutions?
	Are our USPs and/or PODs realistic?
Return on Investment	Is the ROI stated in monetary terms?
	Does the ROI connect back to the Stage One cost?
	Is there a track record of an ROI from previous applications of this solution?
Anecdote	Does the anecdote reference a similar pain or similar solution?
	Are we identifying the customer by name or by sector?
	Do we have a measurable ROI?

Bibliography

Beckwith, Harry. *Selling the Invisible.* New York: Warner Books, 1997.

Cope, Mick. *The Seven Cs of Consulting: The Definitive Guide to the Consulting Process.* London: FT Prentice Hall, 2003.

Krause, Donald G. *The Art of War for Executives.* New York: The Berkley Publishing Group, 1995.

McCormack, Mark H. *What They Don't Teach You at Harvard Business School.* London: Profile Books, 2003

O'Guinn, Thomas, Allen, Chris, Semenik, Richard J. *Advertising and Integrated Brand Promotion.* Boston: South Western Cengage Learning, 2005.

Rock, John. *Key Account Management.* Warriewood, Australia: Business and Professional Publishing, 1998.

Welch, Jack with Welch, Suzy. *Winning.* New York: HarperCollins, 2005.

Wilson, Larry. *Stop Selling, Start Partnering.* New York: John Wiley & Sons, 1995.

Also by Terry Barge

Selling Strategically – A 21st-Century Playbook

In this post-recessionary era, sales professionals in every business-to-business sector must "up their game" significantly in order to create sustainable success for organisations and individuals alike.

Selling Strategically – A 21st-Century Playbook provides a proven and practical journey through the pivotal sales "upgrades" necessary to achieve and sustain revenue growth and profitability in a demanding and highly competitive 21st-century business environment.

This book provides both the "Why?" and the "How?" of "selling strategically" and tracks why this business-to-business sales methodology plays a key role in delivering sales success for forward-thinking organisations. It introduces the role of the Sales Strategist and delves deeply into the four key attributes that define that role.

And to ensure that the book's key sales principles can be applied immediately, there is a unique, step-by-step Playbook that provides the essential "how to" steps.